Eureka!

Challenging **Maths** and **Numerical Reasoning** Exam Questions for **11+** Exam Preparation

The Eureka! 11+ Confidence series

CEM-style Practice Exam Papers covering:
Comprehension, Verbal Reasoning,
Non-Verbal Reasoning and Numerical Reasoning

Numerical Reasoning: Advanced Training Workbooks

Tough exam paper questions and detailed explanations of how to tackle them, to increase speed and reduce error.

Verbal Reasoning: Advanced Training Workbooks

The 1000-Word Brain Boost is an intensive course teaching Synonyms, Antonyms, Odd-One-Out, Analogy, Vocabulary and Cloze, in CEM-style exam paper questions. The answer section explains the important subtleties and distintions that many 11+ candidates find challenging.

ISBN-10: 1511607211
ISBN-13: 978-1511607216

First Published in the United Kingdom in 2015 by Eureka! Eleven Plus Exams
Revision dated **7 August 2015**

Eureka! Eleven Plus Exams is grateful to Sian Williams, Leona Bourne and Balbir Lehto.

Please check **www.eureka11plus.org/updates** for any updates or clarifications for this book.
Tutors seeking volume discounts are advised to contact the office email address below.

We are all human and vulnerable to error. Eureka! Eleven Plus Exams is very grateful to any reader who notifies us of any unnoticed error, so we can immediately correct it and provide a tangible reward.

Preparing for 11+ with this book

Pupils approaching the 11+ Examination face many challenges, including lack of time, uncertainty over what is required, and an ever-changing and secretive testing environment.

Plain "mathematics" questions are progressively being replaced with more demanding "numerical reasoning" questions. Selective schools are increasingly interested in not only rote recall of methods but also the ability to understand questions expressed in prose and skilfully apply (sometimes several) mathematical principles to arrive at an answer.

The *Eureka! 11+ Challenging Maths and Numerical Reasoning* series of books to provide focused preparation for pupils and their busy parents. Questions are expressed in words, with the pupils learning the habit of extracting the relevant numbers and key facts. Most questions are multi-part, reflecting the trend in examinations to challenge pupils skills at progressively higher levels as the question unfolds.

These questions are the upper echelon of what is tested at 11+. Although they need only Key Stage 2 concepts, they are challenging because they require good command of multiple skills simultaneously. Pupils, and perhaps even parents, will find very few of these questions to be very easy. Thankfully, the real exam will contain many easier questions, but preparation time is best spent on those which present greater challenges and therefore more learning opportunities.

When answering the questions
- Set yourself a target, e.g. "3 questions in half an hour"
- Underline the key information if the question is lengthy
- Write your working clearly *and in full* so you can check easily

Go through the answers **soon** after doing the questions
- Do not be sad if you have made mistakes: learn from them
- Many questions cover areas where even strong pupils are prone to errors
- Watch out for the Traps described
- Incorporate the Tips into your methods in future
- See if the Method suggested is quicker or less open to error than yours

For any examination, diligent practice, carefully analysing errors, mulling over methods, and developing and testing your own preferred approaches pay enormous dividends.

1

Imagine a new shorthand symbol, ⊚, is introduced. It is defined as the mean of two numbers. For example, 20 ⊚ 30 = 25.

(i)   What is 1 ⊚ 99 ?   Answer _____

(ii)   What is 1 ⊚ 100 ?   Answer _____

(iii) What is 1 ⊚ 101?   Answer _____

(iv)   0 ⊚ x is 500. What is x?   Answer _____

(v)   y ⊚ 2000 is 1800. What is y?   Answer _____

(vi)   On this number line, p and p ⊚ q are marked. Mark q.

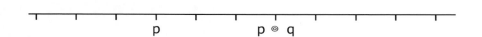

2

School began at the time shown on this image.

That morning, Gavin had English, Drama, breaktime, and then two Maths lessons one after the other. After that came the lunch hour, History, Science and finally Sport.

Each lesson was 45 minutes long, and morning breaktime was 30 minutes.

(i) What time did school finish? Give your answer in the 24 hour clock.

Answer _____

(ii) The minute hand on the clock was 14 cm long. How far had the tip travelled during the duration of the school day? Take π to be 22/7 and give the result *in metres*.

Answer _____ m

(i) Draw a triangle with vertices at (2,-4), (7,-2) and (4,1).

(ii) Draw its reflection in the mirror line shown.

(iii) If the two shapes you have drawn were joined into a single shape, what would the best name for the shape be?

Answer

_____

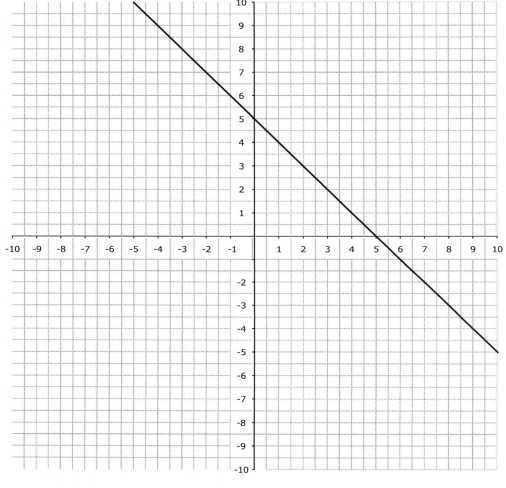

(iv) Draw the shape with vertices at (-5,1), (-5,5), (-2,6) and (-2,2).

(v) Draw its reflection in the mirror line shown.

(vi) What is the area of that reflection?

Answer _____

(i)   Each of the following numbers is the product of two consecutive numbers.
       Write down each pair of consecutive numbers.

    (a)   90   =   _____ × _____

    (b)   132   =   _____ × _____

    (c)   162006 =   _____ × _____

    (d)   930   =   _____ × _____

    (e)   2550   =   _____ × _____

(ii)   Each of the following numbers is the product of three consecutive numbers.
       Write down each triplet of numbers

    (a)   210   =   _____ × _____ × _____

    (b)   26970   =   _____ × _____ × _____

    (c)   999900 =   _____ × _____ × _____

    (d)   9240   =   _____ × _____ × _____

5

(i) Herbert sells 30 cakes for 42 p each and uses this money to buy biscuits for 40 p each.
How much money does Herbert have left over?

Answer _____ p

(ii) Chelsea sets out with a £20 note to buy as many plants as she can for £1·20 each.
She spends the remainder on sweets at 5p each.
She sells the plants at 50% profit, and the sweets at 100% profit.
Express in £ her total profit.

Answer £ _____

(iii) Victoria has only £10 notes. She negotiates a 20% discount for a bulk purchase of 15
plants that would normally have been £1·20 each, and uses all her notes in paying for them.

The change she receives, she spends on plant food at £2 per kilogram. Returning home and
checking on the internet, she finds that each plant requires 300 grams of plant food.

What is the greatest number of her plants that she can feed properly?

Answer _____

Calculate the following

$6·4 ÷ 1·6$ = _____

$4·2 ÷ 0·02$ = _____

$12 ÷ 0·3$ = _____

$3·8 × 0·2$ = _____

$1·9 − 0·02$ = _____

$0·5 × 0·2$ = _____

$12·8 ÷ 0·4$ = _____

$4·9 + 0·19$ = _____

$32·1 − 0·21$ = _____

$0·15 × 8·2$ = _____

$0·3 ÷ 0·015$ = _____

$1·2 × 0·4$ = _____

$13·5 − 0·15$ = _____

$8·1 ÷ 0·27$ = _____

$6·6 ÷ 0·003$ = _____

Plato has drawn out the net below for the outside of a special 12-sided die, whose faces will be numbered 1 to 12.

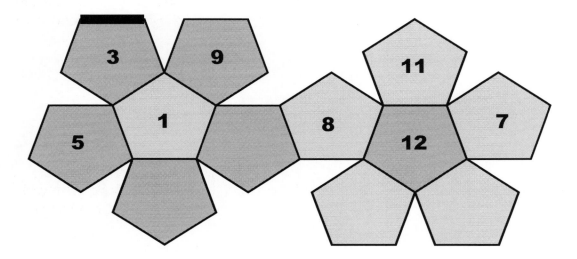

He wants opposite faces of the die to always sum to the same number, 13. He has already labelled the top and bottom faces of the die 1 and 12 respectively, as you can see from the diagram.

(i) Write the missing numbers on the blank faces, to make sure each pair of opposite faces sums to 13. Think about 5 and 8 to help you understand how to find pairs of opposite faces.

(ii) Plato has marked one edge on the net with a thick line. Find the edge which will meet this edge when the net is folded. Mark it with a thick line.

(i) Jordan spends a £50 note at the market on baskets of flowers that are £12 per basket, and the leftover change on plastic stakes at 10p each. She returns to her neighbourhood where she only manages to sell the plastic stakes for 8p each, but successfully sells the baskets of flowers for £15 per basket· How much money does she have at the end of the day?

Total money at end of day = _____

(ii) Four books, each £1·25 normally, are on sale at 20% off. If Mahmoud buys them with a £10 note and spends the rest on as many cakes as he can get at 99 p each, how much change does he finish with?

Change remaining at end = _____

(iii) One summer, Wei Li sets up a lemonade stand, where she sells the drink at £1·20 per 200 ml glass. She makes the drink in a large jug in batches of 3 litres, using each time 24 lemons that she buys at £4·50 per dozen, 300 g of sugar that she buys at £8 per kg.

Assuming she has no other costs, how much profit is she making per day, with sales of 50 glasses of lemonade?

Profit per day = _____

This large square is made up of 21 × 21 smaller squares, each of which is either white, black or grey.

(i) How many of these small squares are grey? Explain your reasoning. Do not attempt to count them all individually.

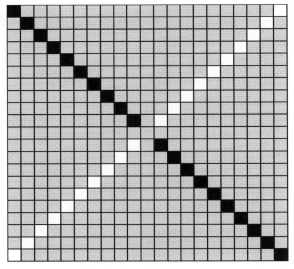

Number of grey squares = _____

(ii) The Sheikh of Abu Karami is pleased with your design, shown above. He commissions you to build a mural with this design, extended to 401 × 401 small squares in size. He wants the black squares to be made of gold, the white squares of silver, and the grey squares of glass.

Gold squares cost £200 each, silver £100 each, and glass £50 each. How much will it cost to buy all the squares needed for the mural?

Cost of squares for the mural = £ _____

Harini lives at 42 Charlton Way. Her friend Mariam lives at number 56 on the same road. All the houses on their side of the road in between their two houses are even-numbered and are owned by families of their friends. Each house (and its garden) is 10 metres wide.

(i) Harini and Mariam can use the back gardens of their houses and of all the houses in between to play. How long is their combined playing space?

Answer _____ m

(ii) Harini flies a kite from her garden. It is pulled by a gust of wind towards Mariam's garden. She runs forward with it but is stopped when she reaches the limit of her own garden. The kite falls only just into Mariam's garden. The string falls across all the gardens between the two houses. How long is the string?

Answer _____ m

(iii) Mariam launches a toy rocket from the centre of her garden. It lands in the centre of Harini's garden. How far has it travelled?

Answer _____ m

11 King Mateo, the first king of Tetron, builds a small castle, the
white square at centre of diagram here. He surrounds it by a very thick
wall, indicated by the black squares. Building the walls
consumes a total of 8 tonnes of rock.

(i) His son, the 2nd King, Fabrizio, adds another layer of wall a
short distance outside the first, to produce the pattern
shown here. How much rock was needed for this layer?

Answer _____ tonnes

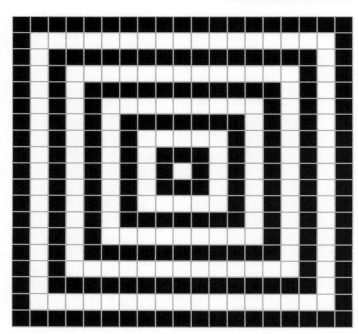

(ii) As the generations pass,
each new king adds a new layer
of wall to the castle complex.
The 5th king, Sergio, brings the
design to the state shown in the
third diagram. How much rock
was needed for this layer?

Answer _____ tonnes

(iii) If this habit continues down
the centuries, which king
(identified by number) will be
the first to use more than 1000
tonnes of rock for the wall that
he adds?

Answer: King number _____

(iv) Each small square is 10 m on its side. The first king's castle complex had an area of 900
m²; the second king's 4900 m². Which king will be the first whose complex has an area
above 1 million square metres?

Answer: King number _____

12

This triangle, which is not drawn to scale, has two sides which are each square numbers.

In fact, they are the squares of consecutive whole numbers.

The triangle's area is 4050 m².

A is an odd number.

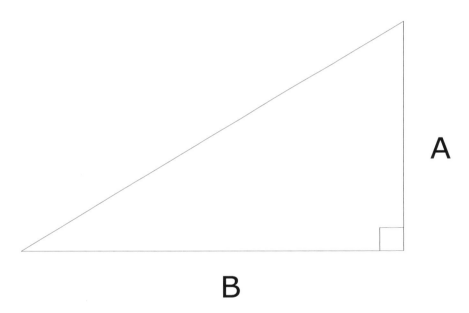

What are A and B?

Answer:

A   =   _____

B   =   _____

13

Idris writes down all the whole numbers from 1 to 1000 inclusive.

(i) How many times did he write the digit 4?

digit 4: _____ times

(ii) How many times did he write the digit 2?

digit 2: _____ times

(iii) How many times did he write the digit 0?

digit 0: _____ times

Jade writes down all the whole numbers from 2000 to 3000 inclusive.

(iv) How many times did she write the digit 4?

digit 4: _____ times

(v) How many times did she write the digit 2?

digit 2: _____ times

(vi) How many times did she write the digit 0?

digit 0: _____ times

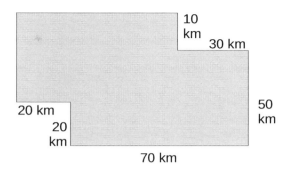

(i) Calculate the area of the tiny nation of Kalgoolistan, whose map is shown here.

Answer _____ km²

(ii) Captain Zara is planning to build a border fence around her country. She is building a test fence as a straight line 1 km long in the desert. She has bought a small batch of ten 100-metre sections of fence, which she will assemble into the test fence. Each fence section needs to be held up by a fencepost at each end. How many fenceposts does she need?

Answer _____ fenceposts

(iii) She is not satisfied with that design of fencing material and tries a different material, which comes in 200-metre sections, again needing to be supported on each side by a fencepost. This time she builds a test fence around a square lake that is 1 km on each side. How many fence sections does she need?

Answer _____ sections

(iv) How many fenceposts does she need for the lake?

Answer _____ fenceposts

(v) Captain Zara decides to fence the entire boundary of Kalgoolistan with a new set of 200-metre sections. How many does she need?

Answer _____ sections

15

Justin throws 3 dice coloured red, green, blue.

(i) What is the lowest total he can throw?

Answer _____

(ii) What is the next-to-lowest total he can throw?

Answer _____

(iii) How many ways can he throw the total you describe in (ii)?

Answer _____

(iv) How many ways can all three dice be thrown?

Answer _____

(v) What is the probability of throwing the total you describe in (ii)?

Answer _____

(vi) What is the probability of throwing a total of 18?

Answer _____

Helen arrives and takes his three dice, and adds a fourth, white, die.
(vii) What is the lowest total she can throw with the 4 dice?

Answer _____

(viii) What is the second-lowest total she can throw?

Answer _____

(ix) How many ways can she throw the total you describe in (viii)?

Answer _____

Toby arrives with 4 further dice. He adds them to the existing 4 dice. He throws all 8 dice.
(x) What is the second-lowest total that Toby can throw?

Answer _____

(xi) Write a formula for the probability of this happening. You may use whole numbers, multiplication signs, division signs and brackets.

Answer _____

16

(i) Ethan and Piotr each buy a car.

Ethan's was on 20% discount, and its original price was half the original price of Piotr's.

If Piotr negotiated a 10% discount so that he only paid £18,000, what price did Ethan pay?

Answer: _____

(ii) Julio sees a shirt for £30 while his sister Keisha sees a dress for £50. They have agreed to spend the same amount of money each on an item of clothing.

Julio manages to get a 20% discount on his shirt.

What percentage discount must Keisha get on her dress for them to each pay the same amount?

Answer: _____

Bob and Jane each ate a fruit.

Consider the following 3 statements, each of which may be true or false.

Statement A

Bob ate an apple and Jane ate a banana or a peach.

Statement B

Jane ate a banana and Bob ate an apple.

Statement C

Bob ate an apple.

(i) Which is most likely to be true?

Answer: Statement _____

(ii) Which is least likely to be true?

Answer: Statement _____

(i) Archie is assembling a cardboard box by folding the kit sketched below.

He has begun labelling the outside surfaces as follows:

U = Up   F = Front   L = Left
D = Down   B = Back   R = Right

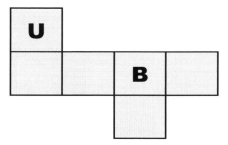

Fill in the letters for the 4 faces he has not yet labelled.

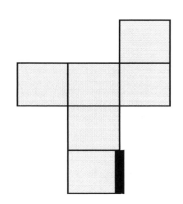

(ii) Oleg is folding the second box. He has marked one edge of one face with a dark line.

Please mark similarly the edge of the face that will meet that line when the box is folded.

(iii) Tokohara is folding the third box, whose volume will be 64 m³.

How far away will the two dots be once the box is folded?

_____ m

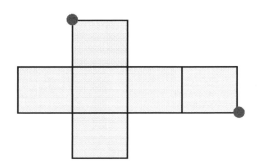

19

A car's position is recorded on a computer system as shown in the following table.

Time (minutes)	0	1	2	3	4	5
Position (m)	3	5	7	9	11	13

(i) Plot the graph of its position against time.

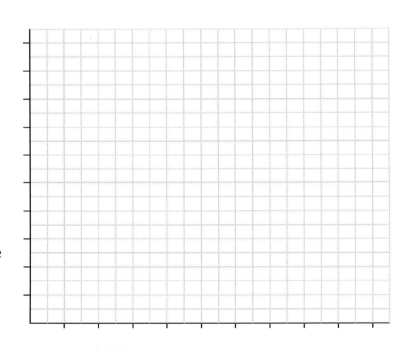

(ii) At what time, in minutes and seconds, did it pass through position 5·5 m?

_____ min _____ sec

(iii) If the position in m of the the car is denoted y, and the time in minutes is denoted t, write a formula that allows y to be calculated for any chosen value of t.

y = _____

(iv) If it continues at this rate, at what time will it reach 100 m?

_____ min _____ sec

20

Examine this sequence of statements which form a pattern:

$$3^2 - 1^2 = 8$$
$$4^2 - 2^2 = 12$$
$$5^2 - 3^2 = 16$$
$$6^2 - 4^2 = 20$$

(i) Write down the next statement in this pattern.

Answer   _____

(ii) Using the pattern, work out what $106^2 - 104^2$ is, showing your working clearly.

Working:

Answer   _____

(iii) Using the pattern, find a pair of square numbers, n^2 and $(n+2)^2$, whose difference is 400. Express them in the form n^2 and $(n+2)^2$.

Answer   _____

(i) How many cube numbers are there from 1 to 8 million inclusive?

Answer: _____

(ii) How many square numbers are there from 15 to 4000 inclusive?

Answer: _____

(iii) How many multiples of 7 are there from 15 to 4000 inclusive?

Answer: _____

22

(i) Marcia was born on Tuesday 3 June. In her first year, what day of the week was 7 August?

Answer _____

(ii) Slowpoke Server Systems closed down early for Christmas at Thursday 16 December, leaving a cheery message for its customers advising that they would be back to deal with any problems on 10 January. On what day of the week are they returning?

Answer _____

(iii) Gordon's birthday, 12 September, is a Wednesday this year. He is planning to celebrate in advance, sharing a friend's birthday party on 16 July – but what day of the week is that?

Answer _____

(iv) Mehreen was born on 14 January 2003 on a Tuesday. Her friend Nikhil was born several weeks later on 3 March 2003: what day of the week was it?

Answer _____

(v) By coincidence Nikhil's sister Ruby was born on Wednesday 3 March 2004, while Mehreen's brother Suleiman was born on 14 January 2004 – on what day?

Answer _____

23

(i) Hermione has 3 more boxes than Athena, but Athena has half as many as Boris. They put their boxes together and obtain from friends 7 more boxes to make a full "wagon-load" of 50 boxes. Once they have done this, what percentage of the boxes in the full wagon-load comes from Boris?

Answer _____ %

(ii) Giorgio has a third as much money as Carla, but Erica has twice as much money as the two of them put together. They pool their funds to buy a model aeroplane for £105, along with the 5 batteries it needs. Each battery is usually £5 but they obtained a 40% discount. How much money did each person contribute to the total of the purchases?

Answer _____ 130

24

(i) Jennifer is twice the age she was 4 years ago.

How old will she be next year?

Answer _____ years

(ii) Last year Dan was three times as old as he was 11 years ago.

How old is he now?

Answer _____ years

(iii) Matilda is now twice the age of her brother Crispin.

Five years ago, she had noticed that she was *seven* times his age!

What is their age difference now?

Answer _____ years

(i) What is the total shaded area?

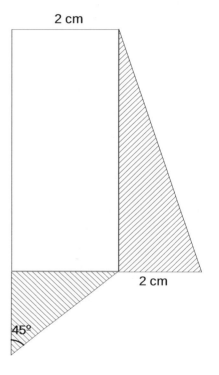

_____ cm²

(ii) What is the area of the rectangle as a proportion of the total area of all 3 shapes?

Proportion = _____

26

For this lawn, which is not drawn to scale, calculate

(i) the perimeter _____ m

(ii) the area _____ m²

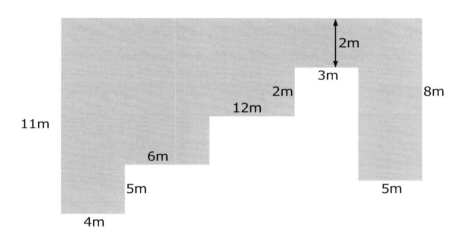

27

An avid fan of the Perry Hatter series, Jemima begs her mother to build a special small bookcase exactly wide enough to hold the entire seven-book series snugly. Each book has 500 pages that are each 1/20th of a millimetre thick, and a front and back cover each 2 mm thick.

(i) How wide should the bookcase be, so that the set of books fits with no spare space?

Answer _____

(ii) While the books are on the shelf as shown below, a minuscule bookworm that had been hiding in the middle of page 1 of the first book begins eating his way through directly towards his fellow bookworm who is located in the middle of the last page of the final book. He eats his way through at 1 mm per minute. If he starts at 13:00 exactly, at what time will he meet the other bookworm?

Time ____:____
     hour min

28

Realising he has let go of his helium party balloon which has floated up to the ceiling, Kevin tries to catch hold of the dangling string. The string is 60 cm long and hangs down from the bottom of the balloon, which is a sphere with radius 10 cm. Even the tips of his outstretched fingers only reach 1·35 m above the ground: he has no chance to reach the ceiling which is 2·8 m high.

He notices the staircase is nearby. Each step on the staircase is 20 cm. How many steps must he ascend before he can just reach the string, if the balloon and string are directly overhead?

Answer: _____ steps

It was frustrating for Ignaz that, just a week before his great exhibition, the caterpillar track treads on his favourite tank in his whole museum had now degraded beyond his many attempts to repair them over the years.

This was the view from the right side of the tank, showing the right tread. On the left of the tank there was another identical tread.

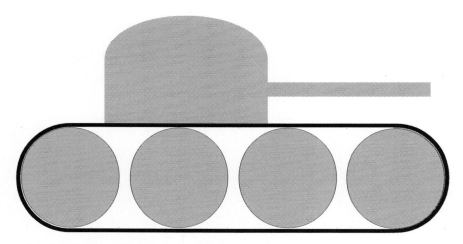

Sighing, he made the call to Tanks R Us. After listening to music on the telephone queue for almost an hour, he reached the chirpy sales assistant. "What total length of tread do you need?"

Ignaz panicked – he hadn't measured the treads and was now out on the street without a calculator. He knew each slender tread surrounded 4 great wheels whose radius was 1·4 m. There was only 30 cm between the rim of each wheel and that of its neighbour.

As the sweat poured down his forehead, he allowed himself to simplify matters by assuming pi was 22/7. He just managed to calculate and order the correct total length of tank tread needed, before his cell phone battery ran out. What was the amount?

Total length of tread needed = _____ m

30

Here are 4 equations:

$$\blacksquare + \blacksquare \qquad = \triangleright + \lozenge$$

$$\lozenge + \triangleright \qquad = \blacktriangledown + \blacktriangledown + \blacksquare$$

$$\lozenge \qquad = \triangleright + 2$$

$$\blacktriangledown \qquad = \left(\blacksquare \div \blacksquare \right) + \left(\triangleright \div \triangleright \right)$$

Each of the symbols $\blacksquare$, $\triangleright$, $\lozenge$ and $\blacktriangledown$ represents a different whole number between 1 and 10 inclusive. Find their values.

$\blacksquare \ = \ \underline{\qquad\qquad}$

$\triangleright \ = \ \underline{\qquad\qquad}$

$\lozenge \ = \ \underline{\qquad\qquad}$

$\blacktriangledown \ = \ \underline{\qquad\qquad}$

Answer **1**

(i) $(1 + 99) \div 2 = 100/2 = $ **50**.

(ii) $(1+100) \div 2 = 101/2 = $ **50·5**.

Or you can write it as "50½".
This question does not specify which form to use.
"50 remainder 1" would be wrong, however.

(iii) $(1+101) \div 2 = 102/2 = $ **51**.

(iv) $(0+x) \div 2 = 500$ means that

$$x/2 = 500$$
$$x \ = \textbf{1000}.$$

(v) $(y+2000) \div 2 = 1800$ means that

$y/2 + 2000/2$	=	1800
$y/2 \ + 1000$	=	1800
$y/2$	=	800
y	=	**1600**.

(vi) Here, the key is to understand that p ⊚ q is always half-way between p and q. If you know where p and p ⊚ q are, place q an equal distance beyond p ⊚ q, on the other side from p.

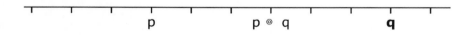

Answer 2

(i)   **Method**

Number of lessons = 2 + 2 + 3 = 7
Time for lessons = 7 × 45 min
                       = 315 min

Total time   = 315 + 30 (breaktime) + 60 (lunch)
                       = 405 min

405 ÷ 60 = 6 remainder 45

Total time = 6 hours 45 min.

Answer: Finish time = **15:45**.

(ii)   **Method**

First calculate how far the tip travels in one hour.

Circumference   = 2 π r
                       = 2 × (22/7) × 14 cm
                       = 44 × 2   by cancelling the "7" and the "14" to "1" and "2".
                       = 88 cm

Then calculate the number of circumferences it travels

Number of turns = 6 + 45/60
                       = 6 ¾

Then calculate what the distance would be

Distance   = 6 ¾ × 88
                       = 6 × 88   +   ¾ × 88
                       = 528   +   66
                       = 594 cm

Answer: Distance = **5.94** m.   (Result must be in metres to gain the mark)

Answer 3

(i) See figure

(ii) **Rhombus**

"Parallelogram" is a valid description of the shape, but is not the *best* description. All four sides are equal.

(iii) See figure

(iv) Area = base × height = 4 × 3 = **12**.

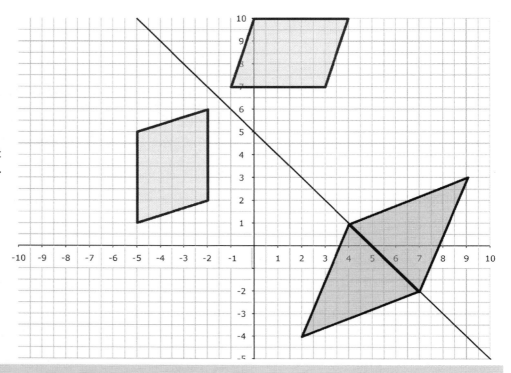

Tip: **Diagonal mirrors**

Step 1 Start with the point nearest the mirror. Imagine walking directly towards the mirror (i.e. in a line perpendicular to the mirror). What do you walk across on the way to the mirror? Do exactly that after you cross the mirror. Here you walk across one small 0·5×0·5 square before the mirror, so do the same after.

Now work methodically around the other corners. Where you have to move horizontally on the original, move vertically on the mirror image; and vice versa.

Step 2 Here, the side labelled "2" is 6 units downwards.

Step 3 So on the mirror image, walk horizontally 6 whole units (journey labelled "3").

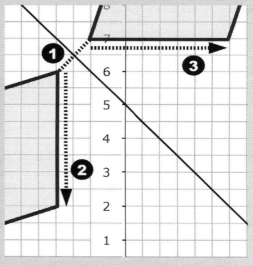

Answer **4**

(i) Pairs

Since the two numbers (A and B) being multiplied are consecutive, their product will be just a little larger than A^2 and just a little smaller than B^2. Think if any numbers, squared, are close to the target value. In the case of 90, 9 and 10 might immediately pop to mind. But if they don't, we can use this as an example of the method. Notice that 90 is close to 81 and to 100, which are the squares of 9 and 10 respectively. Therefore calculate 9 × 10 which comes out to 90.

> (a)   90   =   **9 × 10**

132 should be memorable from your times tables, but if it isn't, you might start from a nearby square number, 100, which is 10 × 10. Working up from there, you might try 10 × 11 = 110, which is not high enough. Next try 11 × 12 = 132

> (b)   132   =   **11 × 12**

Larger numbers can appear more difficult. It helps to have a method for estimating square roots.

Estimating square roots of large numbers

Step 1 Drop **pairs** of digits from the right, until you are down to 1 or 2 remaining digits. For example, to estimate the square root of 495, drop the last two digits, like this: 4[95].

Step 2 Focus on the remaining part, 4, and ask yourself what its square root is, roughly. For 4, this is 2.

Step 3 Now bring back one zero for **every pair** of digits you dropped in Step 1. You dropped one pair so bring back one zero, to get 20. This is your very rough estimate of the square root of 495.

Step 4 Improve your estimate, step by step. 20 squared is 400, which is too small. So try 21 squared: this is 441, still too small. Try 22 squared: 484, still a little under the target. Try 23 squared: 529, which is too large. So you know the square root of 495 is between 22 and 23 (and probably closer to 22).

Try 161604 as a bigger example. If you only dropped one pair of digits, you would be left with 1616[04], and you probably don't want to try to calculate the square root of 1616 in your head. So drop two pairs of digits, to get 16[1604]. The square root of 16 is 4, so now insert two zeros to get 400. This is the first approximation to the square root. You can then try progressively higher numbers until you get as close as you need. 402 turns out to give you exactly the right answer.

However, for this problem you want the pair of consecutive numbers whose product is 162006, so work upwards but use the final digit check to save time, by excluding pairs whose final digits do not fit. 400 × 401 must end in 0, so it is wrong. 401 × 402 must end in 2, so it is wrong. 402 × 403 must end in 6, so is a possibility. Then do the multiplication in full, and you find it is correct.

(c)   162006 =   **402 × 403**

For 930, start by dropping the 30, to get 9[30]. The square root of 9 is 3, and you now need to add one zero back, 3[0], if you wanted a rough estimate of the square root. However we are looking for consecutive factors. 30 × 31 must end in 0, so it is a possibility worth checking. Multiplying it out gives 930, so this is the right answer.

(d)   930   =   **30 × 31**

For 25[50], the square root of 25 is 5, so your first estimate of the square root is 5[0]. Work upwards from here. 50 × 51 must end in 0, so do the full multiplication. A quick way to do this in your head is: 50 × 51 = 50 × 50 + 50 × 1 = 2500 + 50 = 2550.

(e)   2550   =   **50 × 51**

(ii) Triplets

For three consecutive numbers multiplied together, the trick to making the search easier is to be able to estimate cube roots. The cubes of the numbers 1 to 10 are 1, 8, 27, 64, 125, 216, 343, 512, 729 and 1000. One hundred cubed is 1 million.

From the above you will recognise 210 to be close to 6 cubed. Therefore you might try the 3 consecutive numbers that have 6 as their middle element, 5 × 6 × 7 = 30 × 7 = 210.

(a)   210   =   **5 × 6 × 7**

The next number is close to 27000. You can estimate cube roots by the method shown above for square roots, but remember to remove **triplets** of zeros (since 10 cubed is 1000). Write 27[000] whose cube root is 3[0]. So let us try the 3 consecutive numbers centred on 30.

(b)   26970   =   **29 × 30 × 31**

This next number is almost 1 million, i.e. 1[000000], so its cube root is close to 1[00]. Try the 3 consecutive numbers centred on 100.

(c)   999900 =   **99 × 100 × 101**

The final number is 9[240]. 9 is not the cube of a number but is just above 8, which is the cube of 2. So the cube root is close to 2[0]. Try 19 × 20 × 21: 7980, too small. Try 20 × 21 × 22.

(d)   9240   =   **20 × 21 × 22**

Answer 5

The trick to answering these questions is to write down your working clearly so that you can check it.

(i) Working: 30 × 42 p = 1260 p. 1260÷40 = 31 remainder 20.   Answer: **20 p.**

Trap: **Remainders become misleading when you simplify division**

1260÷40 = 31 remainder 20. But if you simplified the division by removing the common factor of 10, for example, and obtained 126÷4, this simplified division has a remainder of only 2: this is not the remainder of the money.

You are free to simplify division by removing common factors, but you *must* then describe any leftovers as a fraction or a decimal.

Example: 26÷8 = 3 remainder 2, or 3¼, or 3·25.
If you reduce it to 13÷4, you get 3 remainder 1, or 3 ¼ or 3·25.

(ii) Working: Number of plants = 2000/120 = 200/12 = 100/6 = 50/3 = 16 2/3, i.e. 16 plants and the leftover money for 2/3 of a plant, which is 2/3 × £1·20 = 80 p.

Leftover money after buying as many items as you can

TOTAL MONEY ÷ ITEM PRICE

One method is to calculate the answer as a whole number and a remainder. The remainder is the leftover money. This can be hard to do if the item price is high.

> e.g. 2000÷120 = 16 remainder 80, i.e. 80p left over.

Alternatively, you can calculate the answer as a fraction or decimal. The fraction or the decimal part is the proportion of the cost of an item that is left over as money.

> e.g. 2000÷120 = (by cancelling) 16 2/3, so the leftover money is 2/3×120 p = 80p.

80p buys 80÷5 = 16 sweets.

Profit on sweets = 100% of total purchase price = 80 p.
Profit on plants = 50% of their total purchase price which was £1·20 × 16, so the profit is £1·20 × 8 = £9·60.
> (This is easier than calculating the full £1·20 × 16 = £19·20 and halving it. It is also easier than calculating the plant sale proceeds of 1·5 × £1·20 × 16 = £28·80, and then subtracting the cost of £19·20. All methods give the same answer, but look for simpler ways so that you leave less room for arithmetical error.)

Her total profit is therefore £0·80 + £9·60 = **£10·40.**

(iii) Cost of plants. This is £1·20 × 15 and then a 20% discount. At first sight, the most obvious way to do this seems to be to calculate 80% × £1·20 × 15 = £0·96 × 15 = £14·40.

However, a moment's thought reveals several choices. It doesn't matter whether you "discount" the price per plant, or the number of plants. 20% of 15 is a round number, 3, offering simpler mental arithmetic: £1·20 × 15, and a 20% discount = £1·20 × 12 = £14·40 (using the 12 times table).

Tip: Simplifying multiplication or division of multiple items

The multiple steps involved create risk for error, so make use of any simplifications that are available. In a chain of numbers being multiplied, A×B×C, it doesn't matter in which order you multiply them, so choose a convenient order.

Example 1:   5×329×2 = 1645×2 = 3290.   This is easier as 5×2×329 = 10×329 = 3290.

Example 2:   25×18×4 = 450×4 = 1800.   This is easier as 25×4×18 = 100×18 = 1800.

In a chain of numbers being multiplied and divided, always cancel wherever possible.

Example 3:   32×15÷8 = 480÷8 = 60.   This is easier as (32÷8)×15 = 4×15 = 60.

Example 4:   (4/9)×(3/40) =(4×3)/(9×40)=12/360=1/30.   This is easier as (4/40)×(3/9)=(1/10)×(1/3)=1/30.

Money left over = £20 - £14·40 = £5·60
Plant food bought = £5·60 ÷ £2·00 = 5·6÷2 = 2·8 kg
Calculated number of plants she can feed properly = 2800 g ÷ 300 g = 28 / 3 = 9 1/3

The examiners want a whole number of plants.
Answer = **9 plants.**

Answer 6

6·4 ÷ 1·6   =   **4**   If you found this difficult, adopt a system such as this:

4 Steps for Multiplying or Dividing Decimals

Step 1 Note where the decimal points are in A and B. How far from the right?

Step 2 Remove the decimal points and do the calculation.

Step 3 Draw the decimal point back in. Start at the right and move leftwards as follows.
If it was multiplication, move the decimal point A + B positions to the left.
If it was division, move the decimal point A **minus** B positions. (If this number of positions is negative, move it rightwards, inserting zeros as you go.)

Step 4 Round the numbers and see if the answer is roughly right, and not out by 10 or 100 fold.

Apply these steps to 6·4 ÷ 1·6. **Step 1** 1 and 1. **Step 2** 64÷16=4. **Step 3** 1-1=0 so put the decimal point at the far right: **Step 4** It is roughly 6 ÷ 2 which is 3, not far from your full answer of 4.

4·2 ÷ 0·02	=	**210.**	Steps: **1** 1 and 2. **2** 42÷2=21. **3** 1-2= -1. **4** 4/0·04=100.
12 ÷ 0·3	=	**40.**	**1** 0 and 1. **2** 12÷3=4. **3** 0-1= -1. **4** 12 divided by a half would be 24.
3·8 × 0·2	=	**0·76.**	**1** 1 and 1. **2** 76. **3** 1+1=2. **4** 4 × 0·2 would be 0·8
1·9 − 0·02	=	**1·88.**	To avoid mix-ups with decimal additions and subtractions, write out the

numbers in full. If they have unequal numbers of digits after the decimal point, add extra zeros to equalise the counts of decimals, as shown below:

$$1·90$$
$$\underline{-\ 0·02}$$
$$1·88$$

0·5 × 0·2	=	**0·1**	**1** 1 and 1. **2** 10. **3** Move left 2, to give 0·10, or 0·1. **4** Half of 0·2 is 0·1.
12·8 ÷ 0·4	=	**32**	
4·9 + 0·19	=	**5·09**	
32·1 − 0·21	=	**31·89**	Hint: write it as 32·10 − 0·21
0·15 × 8·2	=	**1·23**	
0·3 ÷ 0·015	=	**20**	
1·2 × 0·4	=	**0·48**	
13·5 − 0·15	=	**13·35**	
8·1 ÷ 0·27	=	**30.**	**1** 1 and 2. **2** 81÷27 (cancel by 9) = 9÷3=3. **3** 1-2=-1 **4** 9÷0·3 would be 30.
6·6 ÷ 0·003	=	**2200**	**1** 1 and 3. **2** 66÷3=22. **3** 3-1=2 so move the decimal 2 places left, to get

2200. **4** It is roughly 5 divided by 5 thousandths, which would be 1000, so 2200 is reasonable.

Answer 7

(i) and (ii)

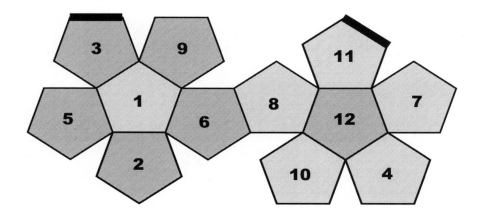

Methods

Opposite faces If you are having difficulty seeing which face is opposite which, look at this diagram in which the 5 is shaded darkest, and its immediate neighbours shaded next darkest, etc. Let's call the "1" side the upper surface, and fold the "12" side downwards.

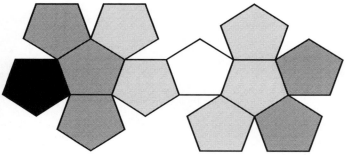

"8", and all polygons to the right of it on the net as drawn above, end up on the underside of the dodecahedron. Note that "8" is on the left hand side of that group of polygons in the net, but ends up on the right hand side of that group once it is folded. The polygons at the top stay at the top after folding (because the folding is right-left, rather than up-down).

Touching edges If you are having difficulty seeing which edge touches which after folding, pick one corner point on the diagram (marked here with a dot) and move away from that point along the perimeter, in both directions, marking the pairs of sides as you go.

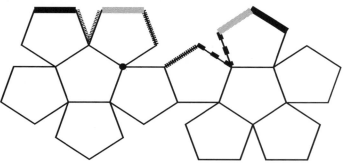

Answer 8

(i)

Calculation for baskets: £50 ÷ £12 = 4 (which would cost £48) remainder £2.

Number of stakes = £2 ÷ 10p = 200/10 = 20.
Money obtained from selling stakes = 20 × 8 p = £1·60.
Money obtained from selling flowers = 4 × £15 = £60
Total money at end of day = £1·60 + £60 = **£61·60**.

(ii)

Cost of books = 4×£1·25×80% = £5× 0·8 = £4.
Money available for cakes = £10 - £4 = £6.
Cakes purchased = 6, each one giving 1p change from a pound.
Change at end = **6p**.

(iii)

Per jug, the cost to Wei Li is:
24×£4·50÷12 = £9 for lemons. (The easiest way to calculate this is 24/12×4·5 = 2×4·5)
300×£8÷1000 = 3×8/10 = £2·40 for sugar.
Total cost for one jug of 3000ml = £11·40.

Cost for one glass of 200 ml = 200/3000×£11·40 = 2/30×11·40 = £0·76
Profit per glass = £1·20 - £0·76 = £0·44.

Profit per day = 50×£0·44 = **£22**.

Answer 9

(i) It is important to follow the instruction not to count the grey squares, for two reasons.

First, some of the marks awarded are for your reasoning, so you should present a mathematical approach that shows understanding, and not simply the end result (which you might simply have obtained by counting).

Second, this first sub-question leads on to a later sub-question which will only be possible if you have developed a mathematical method.

The total number of squares is 21 × 21 = 441. The white and black squares are equal in number, and all the other squares are grey.

One black square is present in every row except the middle row. This means that in the 21 rows there are 20 black squares.
     (This reasoning could equally have been presented with columns instead of rows).

Therefore the total number of grey squares = 441 – 20 black – 20 white = **401**.

(ii) As in many questions of this type, the first part has encouraged you to find the mathematical pattern, to to make it possible to do this later part.

For an n × n pattern, there are n-1 black squares and n-1 white squares. All the remaining squares are grey.

The mural will need:

> 400 gold squares for 400× £200 = £80,000
> *plus*
> 400 silver squares for 400 × £100 = £40,000.
> *plus*
> glass squares.

The number of glass squares will be:
     401×401 – 400 – 400
     = 160801 – 800
     = 160,001.
The cost of the glass squares will therefore be £50 × 160,001
     = £8,000,050.

The total will therefore be **£8,120,050.**

Answer 10

These are dangerous questions because of the fencepost problem.

Fencepost problems

Fences: Suppose you buy 10 ten-metre long sections of fence, to be made into one long fence. Each section of fence must be supported by a fencepost at each end. How many fenceposts do you need?

The answer is **not 10 but 11**. If you consider each fence section to have "it's own" fencepost at its left, then there still needs to be another fencepost at the right of the last fence section.

Holidays: Suppose you are on holiday from 10 August to 15 August inclusive. How many days is that?

The answer is **not 5 but 6**. Although 15 – 10 is 5, this is the number of "changes of day" that occur during the holiday. If each "change of day" is considered to be at the end of a holiday day, there is still an extra holiday day at the end which does not have a "change of day" after it. Therefore the number of holiday days is 15 – 10 + 1 = 6.

To calculate the number of houses, start by calculating the number of steps of 2 in house number between them. This is not the number of houses but the number of "changes of house", $(56 - 42) \div 2 = 7$.

This is also the number of houses between them plus **one** of their own houses (but not both).
If we include the houses of both Harini and Mariam, the number is 8.

(i) Length of playing space = 8 × 10 m = **80 m**.

(ii) The string lies across only the houses *in between*, so its length is 6 × 10 m = **60 m**.

(iii) Launching and landing at an equivalent point in the two gardens makes this a simple calculation. It is the only situation in which you can simply subtract one number from the other.

Distance travelled = 7 changes of house = 7 × 10 m = **70 m**.

Answer **11**

Do not simply count the squares, because later parts of the question need you to understand the pattern.

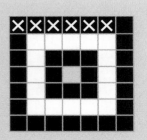

Tip: **Two ways to count sizes of patterned layers**

First, consider each layer of wall to be made of 4 equal segments (which in turn are made of a string of small squares). To avoid double-counting any small squares, it is important to count, in each wall segment, one corner square but not the other. This sketch shows one wall segment (marked with crosses) containing 6 squares.

Second, when a wall layer is added, it can be imagined as a solid (filled-in) black square, with its insides (a square whose side is smaller than the wall by 2 units) scooped out.

Applying the first method, the total for the 1st layer is 4 × 2 = 8 black squares. The 2nd layer is 4×6=24 black squares. For every new king, the length of each wall segments becomes **4 longer**, because on each side there are 2 new white squares and 2 new black squares.

The formula for this must increase by 4 for every increase in the king number (which we can call k) and therefore will have the form "4 k plus (or minus) something". To find out what the "something" is, pick any row (for example, the top row) and see what the "something" would have to be. 2 = 4×1 plus or minus what? Minus 2.

King number, k	Length of wall segment	Length of whole wall layer
1	2	8
2	6	24
3	10	40
4	14	56
k	4 k – 2	16 k – 8

The second method is as follows:

King number, k	Full length of side	Outer area	Area scooped out	Wall area of this layer
1	3	3×3	1×1	9 – 1 = 8
2	7	7×7	5×5	49 – 25 = 24
3	11	11×11	9×9	121 – 81 = 40
k	4 k – 1	$(4k-1)^2$	$(4k-3)^2$	$(4k-1)^2 - (4k-3)^2$

Wall area is more complicated to work out by this second method:

$$(4k-1)^2 - (4k-3)^2$$

$$= (16k^2 - 8k + 1) - (16k^2 - 24k + 9)$$
$$= 16k - 8$$

This is why it can be useful to explore more than one solution approach.

(i) Second king, **8 tonnes**.

(ii) Fifth king, $16 \times 5 - 8 = $ **72 tonnes**.

(iii) Solve

$$16k - 8 = 1000$$
$$\Longrightarrow \quad 16k = 1008$$
$$\Longrightarrow \quad k = 1008 \div 16 = 63. \text{ Answer: the } \mathbf{63^{rd}} \textbf{ king.}$$

(iv) Make life easy for yourself. To avoid calculating numbers approaching a million, make use of the fact that each small square is $10 \times 10m = 100 \text{ m}^2$. The number of small squares needed is therefore 1 million / 100 = 10,000.

From either of the calculation methods above, the entire side is 4k-1 long. So solve:

$$(4k - 1)^2 = 10,000. \qquad \text{Take square roots on both sides:}$$
$$4k - 1 = 100$$
$$4k = 101$$
$$k = 25 \tfrac{1}{4}, \text{ which is not a whole number.}$$

To decide what to give as the answer, note that the 25th king will not have a large enough area, so the answer is the **26th king**.

Answer **12**

The challenge in this type of question is applying knowledge from different branches of mathematics in a single question.

A and B are each square numbers. Let us call the numbers of which they are the squares, c and d. Then
        $A = c^2$ and
        $B = d^2$.

The area of the triangle is ½ A B. This means

$(½) c^2 d^2$	=	4050
$c^2 d^2$	=	8100

It might leap out at you that c^2 could be 81 and d^2 could be 100, i.e. c = 9 and d = 10.

However, in general, look out for two traps.

- Could they be the other way round?

    The question might force one ordering in various ways, for example, by indicating that A<B.

- Could there be other solutions?

    Although there are other solutions to $c^2 d^2$ = 8100, none of them have c^2 and d^2 close enough to each other to be meet the requirement in the question, that they be squares of consecutive numbers.

Answer:
        A is 81
        B is 100

Answer 13

It is important to have a method for questions of this type, and to beware the four big traps:
- missing a whole group of ways the digit can appear
- double-counting the same digit
- careless counting at the beginning or end of the range
- ignoring an important word such as "odd" or "even"

Suppose the range is 1 to 1000. To be systematic, break down this range into two parts. The first part consists of numbers of the pattern ■ ■ ■ , where each ■ represents a digit; the second part is the number 1000 which does not fit the pattern as it has a 4th digit.

Step 1. Consider the pattern ■ ■ ■ . Although each digit can be from 0 to 9, leading zeros are not written, i.e. 007 is written as blank blank 7, and (b) the question starts the range at 1, so 000 is not included.

Step 2. Consider the last digit: ■ ■ [■]. This has 10 possible values, 0 to 9. For each last-digit value from 1 to 9 there are 10 possible values for the first digit and 10 for the second digit, i.e. 100 possibilities. This means **each of the digits 1 to 9 appears in the last position 100 times.** The digit 0 is an exception, appearing 99 times because 0 0 0 is missing from the range.

Step 3. Consider the middle digit: ■ [■] ■. Again, each middle-digit value from 1 to 9 appears 100 times. The digit 0 would appear 99 times if leading zeros are written, but since they are not (i.e. 001 to 009 appear as just 1 to 9) , the zero appears only 99 – 9 = 90 times.

Step 4. Consider the first digit: ■ [■] ■. Again, each first-digit value from 1 to 9 appears 100 times. The digit 0 is never written in this position in the pattern ■ ■ ■.

Step 5. Check the full range again, and look for restrictions like "odd" or "even". This question asked for the range to go to 1000 *inclusive.* We did not cover 1000 in the pattern ■ ■ ■above, so there is an extra occurrence of the digit 1, and 3 extra occurrences of the digit 0.

Totals. Each of the digits 2 to 9 appear 300 times. 0 appears 99 + 90 + 0 + 3 = 192 times. 1 appears 301 times.

Answers
(i) digit 4: **300** times
(ii) digit 2: **300** times
(iii) digit 0: **192** times

For the range 2000 to 3000 inclusive, there is now no need to think about leading zeros not being written, since the first digit is in almost all cases 2. Think of this as 1000 numbers with the pattern 2 ■ ■ ■, and one extra number, 3 0 0 0.
(iv) digit 4: **300** times
(v) digit 2: **1300** times
(vi) digit 0: **303** times

Answer 14

(i) First, fill in the two missing dimensions (shown in bold here). For example, if the top horizontal length is x, then x + 30 must equal the two horizontal sections on the bottom = 20+70, i.e. x=90 − 30 = 60.

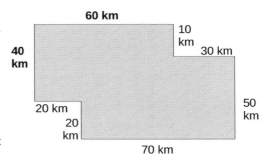

One way to calculate the grey area is to break it into 3 rectangles, and add up their areas. *An easier way* is to calculate the area of an imaginary rectangle around the country, 90×60 = 5400 km², and subtract the two "bites" at bottom left (20 × 20 = 400 km²) and top right (10 × 30 = 300 km²). Area of country = **4700 km²**.

(ii) **11 fenceposts**. This is the notorious fencepost problem.

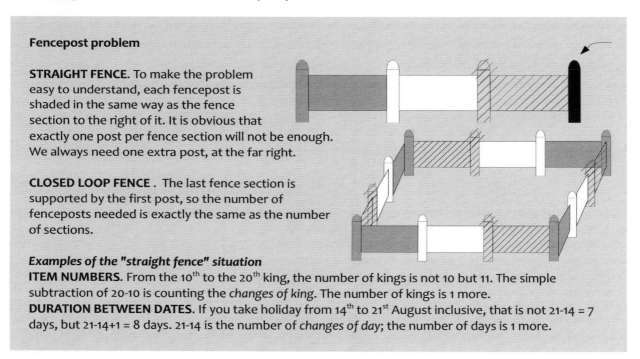

Fencepost problem

STRAIGHT FENCE. To make the problem easy to understand, each fencepost is shaded in the same way as the fence section to the right of it. It is obvious that exactly one post per fence section will not be enough. We always need one extra post, at the far right.

CLOSED LOOP FENCE . The last fence section is supported by the first post, so the number of fenceposts needed is exactly the same as the number of sections.

Examples of the "straight fence" situation
ITEM NUMBERS. From the 10th to the 20th king, the number of kings is not 10 but 11. The simple subtraction of 20-10 is counting the *changes of king*. The number of kings is 1 more.
DURATION BETWEEN DATES. If you take holiday from 14th to 21st August inclusive, that is not 21-14 = 7 days, but 21-14+1 = 8 days. 21-14 is the number of *changes of day*; the number of days is 1 more.

(iii) The perimeter is 4 km. Number of **fence sections** = 4000/200 = **20**.

(iv) Since this is a closed loop, **number of fenceposts = 20**.

(v) Number of fence sections = perimeter ÷ fence section length = 300 km ÷ 0·2 km = **1500**.

Answer **15**

(i)   **3.**

(ii)   **4.**

(iii)   **3.**   (He could throw R2 G1 B1 or R1 G2 B1 or R1 G1 B2)

(iv)   **216.**   (Each die has 6 possibilities. 6 × 6 × 6 = 216)

(v)   **3/216 or 1/72 .**

(vi)   **1/216.**   (Since all 3 dice would have to show a 6)

(vii)   **4.**

(viii)   **5.**

(ix)   **4.**

Method:

R	G	B	W
1	1	1	2
1	1	2	1
1	2	1	1
2	1	1	1

(x)   **9.**

(xi)   **8 ÷ (6 × 6 × 6 × 6 × 6 ×6 × 6 × 6).**

Explanation:

The numerator is the number of ways of achieving what was wanted. Exactly one die has to be a "2", with all others being "1"s. There are 8 choices of die to be a "2", so there are 8 ways.

Meanwhile the denominator is the total number of ways of throwing these dice. Each of the 8 dice have 6 sides, so the denominator has eight 6's multiplied together.

Answer 16

(i) Work from the part of the puzzle where most is known: Piotr's.

Trap: **What was the price before the discount?**

Do not make the mistake of trying to undo an X% discount by adding X%. To see why it never works, imagine a price was discounted by 90% from £1 to £0·10. A later 90% increase, on this new lower value, only raises the price to £0·19, not the original £1. This is because the reduced price is smaller, so the same percentage change is fewer pence.

The correct approach is to recognise that after an X% discount, the price is 100-X% of its original price.

Piotr paid £18,000 which was 90% of the original price. Therefore 10% of the original price was £2,000 and the whole original price was £20,000.

Ethan's car originally had a price half that of Piotr's, which means £10,000, but he obtained a 20% discount, so he paid **£8,000**.

(ii) Julio pays 80% of £30 = £24. Keisha must obtain a reduction of £50-£24 = £26, which is **52%**.

Answer **17**

This question is about logic and not about calculating an exact probability.

> **For X and Y to occur together, X must occur and Y must occur**
>
> In general, a statement requiring X to happen and making no remark about Y, is more likely to be true than one that requires both X and Y.
>
> This extends to 3 or more independent events (X, Y, Z etc). "X and Y" is more likely to be true than "X and Y and Z".
>
> Remember that demanding that an event not occur is just as restrictive as demanding that it does occur. So "X" is more likely to be true than "X and not Y".

(i)   **C**

Method

For all 3, Bob has to eat an apple.
For C, nothing else is required: Jane can eat what she wants.
Therefore C can most easily happen.

(ii)   **B**

Method

It must be A or B.
The difference between them is that in A Jane is allowed to eat either a banana or a peach, while in B she has to eat a banana.
B is most restrictive, and therefore is least likely to be true.

Answer **18**

Trap: **Inside or outside? It can matter**

While sometimes you can answer questions about nets without knowing whether you are looking at the inside or the outside, at other times, especially when labelling the faces, it is crucial to know.

The question makes clear that we are looking at the outside of the net. If you mistakenly assumed it was the inside of the net, you would put the labels for R and L the wrong way round in part (i).

(i)

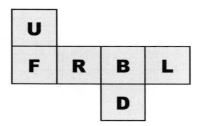

(ii)
Many students try to do this in their heads and run into trouble. It is better to draw a sketch of the folded shape (as shown on the right) which will help obtain the correct answer.

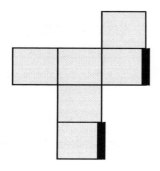

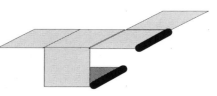

(iii) **4 m.**

Explanation.

Since the volume of the cube is 64 m³, its side must be the cube root of this which is 4 m. During folding, the two points labelled "1" come together, and then the two points labelled "2" come together. This means the upper dot, which is at 2, is only one side-length away from the lower dot.

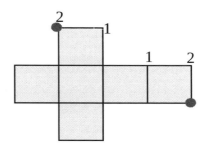

Answer 19

(i) The graph should look like this.

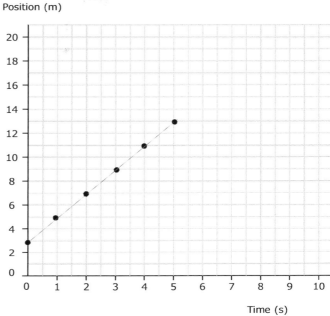

(ii) **1 min 15 sec**
This can be estimated from the graph but it is better to calculate it directly. The distance is ¼ of the way from 5 m to to 7 m, so calculate the time ¼ of the way from 1 min to 2 min.

(iii) **y = 2 t + 3**

Method: Observe in the table that for every increase in t of 1 unit, the value of y increases by 2. This means the formula must be y = 2 t + a constant (let's call it k).

Now find the constant k using any of the (t,y) pairs in the table. For example, using the initial pair, 3 = 2 × 0 + k, which means k= 3. Therefore y = 2 t + 3.

(iv) **48 min 30 sec**

Method: Solve   100   = 2 t + 3
=>   97   = 2 t
=>   48·5   = t

Answer 20

(i) $7^2 - 5^2 = 24$

(ii)   The pattern available is as follows:
   $3^2 - 1^2 = 8$
   $4^2 - 2^2 = 12$
   $5^2 - 3^2 = 16$
   $6^2 - 4^2 = 20$
   $7^2 - 5^2 = 24$

The first and second columns each contain a number that advances by 1 from each row to the next, while the third column advances by 4. So you are looking for a formula that might have the form:
   $(n + \text{constant})^2 - (n + \text{constant})^2 = 4n + \text{constant}$
The number in the second column happens to be the same as the row number of the pattern, so let's call that n. This gives
   $(n + 2)^2 - n^2 = 4n + 4$

For the question " $106^2 - 104^2$" we should use n=104.
   $106^2 - 104^2 = 4 \times 104 + 4$
   $= 416 + 4$
   $= 420$

(iii)   If we want $(n+2)^2$ and n^2 to differ by 400, then according to the equation above,
   $400 = 4n + 4$
   $100 = n + 1$
   $n = 99$

The question asked for the smaller of the two to be listed first. So:

The pair of squares is 99^2 and 101^2.

Answer 21

(i) The cubes of the numbers 1 to 10 are 1, 8, 27, 64, 125, 216, 343, 512, 729 and 1000. 100 cubed is 1 million.

If the question had asked how many cube numbers there were from 1 to 1 million, you could start by noting that one cubed is 1 and 100 cubed is 1 million. So in between 1 and 100 the numbers' cubes lie between 1 and 1 million, and therefore there are exactly 1000 cube numbers from 1 to 1 million.

8 million is 8 times 1 million, i.e. $2^3 \times 100^3$. This means it is the cube of $2 \times 100 = 200$ Therefore the number of cubes from 1 to 8 million inclusive = **200**.

(ii) Use the same trick for the square numbers: map the wide range back into the square roots which are sequential numbers and therefore easy to count.

Step 1 In the range 15 to 4000, which is the *smallest* square number? You should instantly recognise the answer to be $16 = 4^2$.
Step 2 In the range 15 to 4000, which is the *largest* square number? Estimate the square root of 4000, as follows. 40[00]. 40 is between 36 (which is 6^2) and 49 (which is 7^2). So try half way: 65. 65^2 turns out to be 4225, over the limit, so work down. $64^2 = 4096$, again over. $63^2 = 3969$, which is now inside the range.
Step 3 What is the range of whole-number square roots to which you are mapping the square numbers 15 to 4000? From 4 to 63. All those square roots (and no others) have squares between 5 and 4000.
Step 4 How many are there? Be careful: it is not 63-4 = 59, but 63-4+1 = 60, because both 4 and 63 are valid numbers. Number of squares between 15 and 4000 = **60**.

(iii) **Step 1** 15÷7 = 2 and a remainder.

Step 2 4000÷7 = 571 and a remainder.

Step 3 So the whole-number results of division will run from 3 to 571.

Step 4 This is a total of 571-3+1 = 569. Number of multiples of 7 in the range 15 to 4000 = **569**.

Trick: **Mapping a thinly-populated, wide range back into a small, dense range**

The cube numbers are widely spread out and impossible to count manually, but their underlying cube roots are densely packed (all adjacent to each other) and therefore easy to count. By working with the neatly ordered cube roots, your task of counting has become much easier.

Answer **22**

Tip: **Solving day-of-the-week puzzles**

Step 1 Know how many days there are in each month. One way is the rhyme, "30 days has September, April, June and November. All the rest have 31, except February...". February is 29 days on leap years and 28 days on all other years.

Step 2 Sketch a minimalist calendar, as shown below.

Step 3 Write only what is needed, as shown in the example below.

(i) Sketch a chart as shown below.

Month	Date	Day name	
June	3	Tue	
	10		<---- No need to write day for steps of 7 days,
	17		because it does not change
	24	Tue	<---- When going one-day-at-a-time,
	25	Wed	always write the day names
	26	Thu	
	27	Fri	
	28	Sat	
	29	Sun	
	30	Mon	
July	1	Tue	
	8		
	15		
	22		
	29	Tue	<---- If the next +7 would take you past the
	30	Wed	end of the month, go one by one and write
	31	Thu	the day names
Aug	1	Fri	
	8	Fri	

Mark any change ------> of month

7th August is therefore a **Thursday**.

(ii) **Monday.**

(iii) The method can equally run in reverse. Start at the bottom and work upwards, subtracting 7's until you reach your target or get too close to the beginning of the month.

Month	Date	Day name
Jul	**16**	**Mon**
	17	Tue
	24	Tue
Jul	31	Tue
Aug	1	Wed
	2	Thu
	3	Fri
	10	
	17	
	24	
Aug	31	Fri
Sep	1	Sat
	2	Sun
	3	Mon
	4	Tue
	5	Wed
Sep	**12**	**Wed**

--> Result comes out here: **Monday**

<------ **START HERE** for question (iii)

(iv)

Month	Date	Day name
Jan	**14**	**Tue**
	21	
	28	Tue
	29	Wed
	30	Thu
Jan	31	Fri
Feb	1	Sat
	8	Sat
	15	Sat
	22	Sat
	23	Sun
	24	Mon
	25	Tue
	26	Wed
	27	Thu
Feb	28	Fri
Mar	1	Sat
Mar	2	Sun
Mar	**3**	**Mon**

<--- 2003 is not a leap year, so there is no 29 Feb

---> **Result**

(v) The dates again are 14 January and 3 March, but 2004 is a leap year, and therefore there is a 29th February and so one more day between these dates.
Therefore the period, which ends on a Wednesday this year, also begins on a **Wednesday**.

Answer 23

These puzzles are easily solved with algebra. The trick is to make sure you know which variable is which. For example, if people's first names start with different letters, use those initial letters. Always list the variables for your benefit.

(i)   H = Hermione
         A = Athena
         B = Boris

         H = A + 3   ----------- Equation (1)
         A = B ÷2   ----------- Equation (2)
         H + A + B = 50 − 7 = 43   ----------- Equation (3)
Equations (1) and (2) allow us to rewrite equation 3 in terms of A only:
         (A+3) + A +(2 A) = 43
=>   4 A + 3 = 43
=>   4 A   = 40
=>   A   = 10

Using (2),   B   = 20.   Answer: Boris' contribution = 20÷50 = **40%.**

(ii)   G = Giorgio
         C = Carla
         E = Erica

         G = C / 3, or, equivalently, C = 3 G   ----------- Equation (1)
         E = 2 (G + C)   ----------- Equation (2)
         E + G + C = £105 + 5×60%×£5 = £120   ----------- Equation (3)

Applying (1) to (2),
         E = 2 (G + 3G) = 8 G.
Applying this to (3)
         8G + G + 3G = £120
            12 G   = £120
             G   = £10   **Giorgio contributed £10**
                                 Carla contributed £30
                                 Erica contributed £80

Answer 24

> Make sure to keep straight the different times at which age is calculated. A simple convention is to have a variable for the age now, and use offsets of this for ages in the past or the future. If there is more than one person, you might use their initials to mean their ages now.

(i) Let n = age now

$$n = 2(n-4)$$
$$n = 2n - 8$$

Rearranging, $8 = n$

Age next year = **9 years.**

(ii) Let n = age now

$$n - 1 = 3(n - 11)$$
$$n - 1 = 3n - 33$$
$$32 = 2n$$
$$n = 16$$

Age now = **16 years.**

(iii) Let m = Matilda's age now
          c = Crispin's age now

$$m = 2c \qquad \text{---- Equation (1)}$$
$$m - 5 = 7(c - 5) \qquad \text{---- Equation (2)}$$

Applying (1) to (2),

$$2c - 5 = 7(c - 5)$$
$$2c - 5 = 7c - 35$$
$$30 = 5c$$
$$c = 6$$

By (1)

$$m = 12$$

Answer: **Age difference = 6 years.**

Answer **25**

Calculations are as shown on the figure.

It is necessary to notice the 45° angle at the bottom left. Since one other angle of the triangle is 90°, the remaining angle must be 180 − 90 − 45 = 45°.

That two angles are identical (45°) means the two sides are also identical. This tells us that the vertical side is, like the horizontal side, 2 cm.

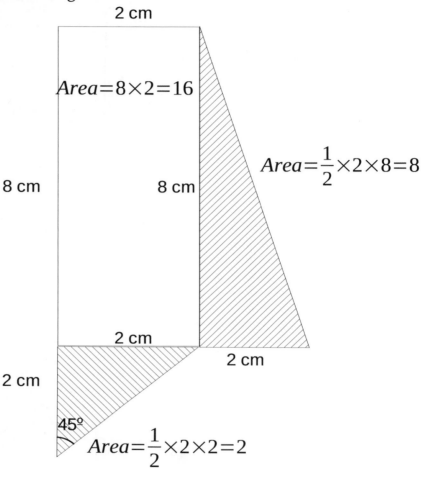

(i)

Total shaded area
= 8 + 2
= **10 cm²**.

(ii)

Area of rectangle as a proportion of the total of all 3 shapes

= 16 ÷ (16 +10)
= 16 / 26
= **8 / 13**

Answer **26**

(i) Perimeter = **94 m.**

Method. Calculate the lengths for the 3 sides where it is not stated, as shown below.

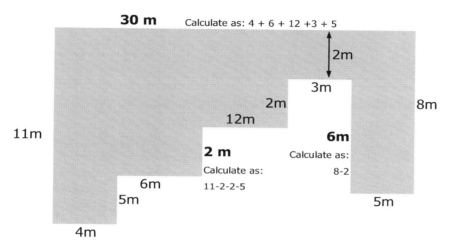

(ii) Area = **174 m².**

Method. Break into rectangles and sum their areas.

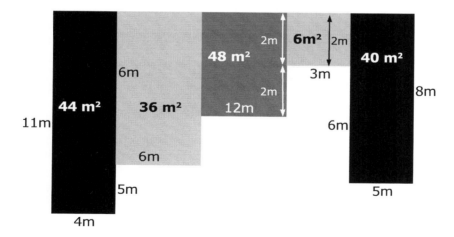

Answer 27

> **Tip: Make multiplication easy if you can**
>
> You can calculate the thickness of the pages inside a book in two ways:
> (a) $500 \times (1/20) = 500 \div 20 = 50/2 = 25$
> (b) $500 \times (1/20) = 500 \times 0.05 = 25.00$
>
> Approach (b), converting to a decimal, is more difficult because there is risk of making a mistake in converting 1/20 to 0.05, and again risk of making a mistake when placing the decimal into the result of 500×0.05.
>
> If the multiplication can be made easy, as in Approach (a), it will be quicker and less error prone. Much of the exam is about avoiding error, so choose methods with fewer risky steps.

(i) Each book's thickness is $500 \times (1/20) + 2 \times 2 = 25 + 4 = 29$ mm
For the 7-book series this is $29 \times 7 = $ **203 mm.**

(ii) Method. The first page of the first book is not the leftmost page on the bookshelf, and the last page of the last book is not the rightmost, as shown on the diagram below.

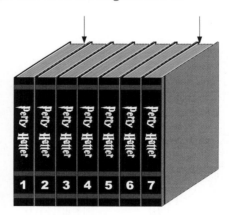

Therefore the bookworm can omit not only the back cover of book 1 and the front cover of book 7, but also all 1000 pages in those two books. The distance it has to eat through is therefore not 203 mm but shorter, by $2 + 2 + 1000 \div 20 = 54$ mm. Distance = $203 - 54 = 149$ mm. This takes 149 minutes, which is 2 hours and 29 minutes.

Time: **15:29**

Answer 28

The gap needing to be closed by the 20 cm steps is 280 – 80 – 135 = 65 cm.

Number of steps needed = 65÷20 = 3 and a bit. The marking scheme will not allow fractional steps. 3 steps will not be enough. Therefore:

Number of steps needed = **4**.

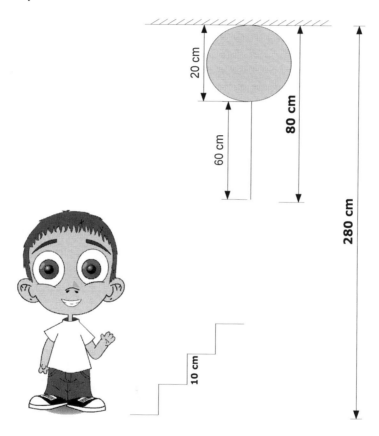

Answer 29

Total length of tread needed = **54·8 m**.

This type of question is deceptively simple. To answer it correctly, all you need to do is avoid the various traps.

- When the size of a circle or sphere is given, pay attention to whether it is the *radius* or the *diameter*.
- Watch out for sizes given in two different units: on your diagram use a *single, consistent* unit.
- When there are a series of objects, don't assume you can mentally keep track of their sizes and positions. Mark them on your diagram.
- Use symmetry to simplify calculations, but ensure you multiply up for all the symmetries at the end.

Method

The half circumference (shown dotted at the left of the figure below) plus the top flat part of the track have a length of 4·4 + 1·4 + 2·8×2 + 1·4 + 0·3×3 = 13·7 m. These have identical counterparts at the right of the figure plus the bottom flat part of the track. For the track seen on this view of the tank has length 2 × 13·7 = 27·4 m.

Remember this is only one side of the tank: there is another identical track on the other side of the tank.

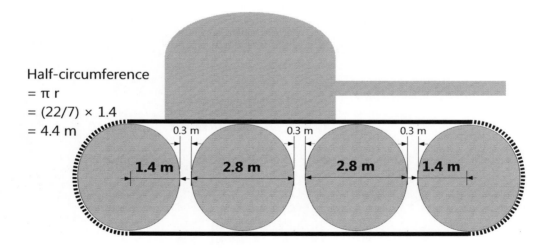

View of tank from the right.

Answer 30

$$▨ = 4 \qquad ▷ = 3 \qquad ◊ = 5 \qquad ▼ = 2$$

Method Number the equations in the question (1) to (4).

Equation (4) is the most useful to start with. Any[*] number divided by itself gives 1, therefore

$$▼ = (▨ ÷ ▨) + (▷ ÷ ▷) = 1+1 = 2$$

Equations (1) and (2) have the interesting feature that $◊ + ▷$ appears in both, i.e. the right of (1) is identical to the left of (2). Therefore the left of (1) must equal the right of (2), i.e.

$$▨ + ▨ = ▼ + ▼ + ▨$$

which, by cancelling out one $▨$ on each side, gives

$$▨ = ▼ + ▼ = 2 + 2 = 4$$

Equation (3) gives a formula for $◊$ in terms of $▷$, that can then be substituted into the final unused equation, (2):

$$▷ + 2 \quad + ▷ \quad = ▼ + ▼ + ▨$$

$$\Rightarrow \quad 2\,▷ + 2 \quad = 8$$

$$\Rightarrow \quad ▷ \quad = 3$$

Finally, applying equation (3),

$$◊ \quad = 5$$

[*] Note: "Any number", except for zero. The question makes clear that none of the symbols is zero.

6461102R00041

Printed in Germany
by Amazon Distribution
GmbH, Leipzig